Flint River

by Amelia J. Pohl

STATE
STANDARDS
PUBLISHING®

Your State • Your Standards • Your Grade Level

Dear Educators, Librarians and Parents . . .

Thank you for choosing the *"Georgia, My State"* Series! We have designed this series to support the Georgia Department of Education's Georgia Performance Standards for elementary level Georgia studies. Each book in the series has been written at appropriate grade level as measured by the ATOS Readability Formula for Books (Accelerated Reader), the Lexile Framework for Reading, and the Fountas & Pinnell Benchmark Assessment System for Guided Reading. Photographs and/or illustrations, captions, and other design elements have been included to provide supportive visual messaging to enhance text comprehension. Glossary and Word Index sections introduce key new words and help young readers develop skills in locating and combining information.

We wish you all success in using the *"Georgia, My State"* Series to meet your student or child's learning needs. For additional sources of information, see www.georgiaencyclopedia.org.

Jill Ward, President

Publisher
State Standards Publishing, LLC
1788 Quail Hollow
Hamilton, GA 31811
USA
1.866.740.3056
www.statestandardspublishing.com

Library of Congress Cataloging-in-Publication Data
Pohl, Amelia J., 1984-
   Flint River / by Amelia J. Pohl.
      p. cm. -- (Georgia, my state. Rivers)
   Includes index.
   ISBN-13: 978-1-935077-55-8 (hardcover)
   ISBN-10: 1-935077-55-4 (hardcover)
   ISBN-13: 978-1-935077-62-6 (pbk.)
   ISBN-10: 1-935077-62-7 (pbk.)
   1. Flint River (Ga.)--Description and travel--Juvenile literature. I. Title.
   F292.F57P64 2009
   917.58'90444--dc22

                              2009036091

Printed in the United States of America, North Mankato, Minnesota, October 2009, 070209.

About the Author

Amelia Pohl is a graduate of the University of Georgia's noted Grady College of Journalism and Mass Communication, one of the oldest and most distinguished communication programs in the country. She is a graduate of the Grady at Oxford, England, program of study and is a member of the National Scholars Honor Society. She lives in Athens, Georgia.

Table of Contents

The Flint River starts as groundwater.

Appalachian Plateau

Blue Ridge Mountains

Valley and Ridge

Piedmont

★ Atlanta

Hartsfield-Jackson International Airport

Flint River

Upper Coastal Plain

Lower Coastal Plain

The Flint River starts near the Atlanta airport.

Let's Explore!

Hi, I'm Bagster! Let's explore the Flint River! It starts near the Atlanta airport in the Piedmont region. The Flint River begins as **groundwater**. Groundwater is water that is under the ground. It seeps up to the surface. Creeks and streams add water to the river. It gets bigger.

The Flint tumbles fast over the fall line!

Appalachian Plateau

Blue Ridge Mountains

Valley and Ridge

Piedmont

★ Atlanta

Sprewell Bluff

Fall Line

Flint River

Upper Coastal Plain

Lower Coastal Plain

The Flint flows freely at Sprewell Bluff.

A Free River!

The Flint flows freely. It is clean and **natural**. People have not changed it. It tumbles over **shoals**. These are shallow and rocky places in a river. It flows to Sprewell Bluff. A **bluff** is an area of high land. It crosses the **fall line**. This is an area of land that falls steeply. The water falls 70 feet in two miles! That's fast!

The river twists and turns like an S.

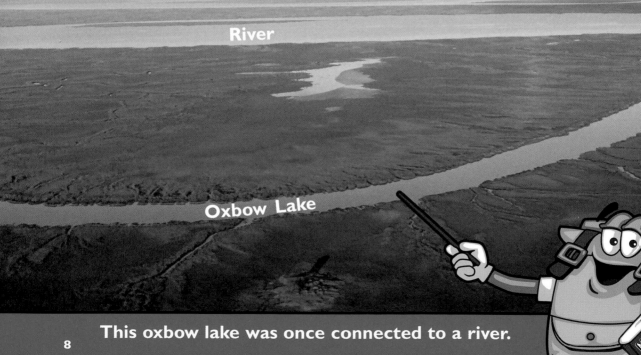

River

Oxbow Lake

This oxbow lake was once connected to a river.

Twisting and Turning

The Flint flows south into the Coastal Plain region. The land is flat and sandy here. The river becomes deep and wide. It moves slowly. It begins to twist and turn like an *S*. Sometimes, the curves get cut off. They form **oxbow lakes**. These lakes are curved like horseshoes.

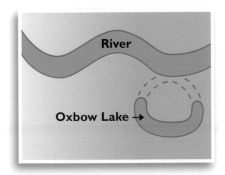

Wetlands form in the floodplains.

Roads and towns can get flooded in a floodplain!

Land floods in a floodplain when it rains a lot.

Floodplains, Wetlands, and Swamps

There are big **floodplains** around the Flint. These areas flood with water when it rains a lot. They form **wetlands** and **swamps**. These are areas of land that are covered in water all or part of the time. They help clean the water. Sometimes, towns and roads get flooded, too!

Lake Blackshear is on the Flint River.

The ground below Albany is limestone.

Appalachian Plateau

Blue Ridge Mountains

Valley and Ridge

Piedmont

⭐ Atlanta

Upper Coastal Plain

Flint River

Lake ← Blackshear

← Lake Chehaw

Albany

Lower Coastal Plain

Blue hole springs form in the limestone.

Dams, Lakes, and Springs

Dams block the water on the Flint River. The dams make Lake Blackshear and Lake Chehaw. Then the Flint flows to Albany. The ground here is **limestone**. This is a type of rock. **Caves** or holes in the limestone fill with groundwater. They make **blue hole springs**. The water bubbles to the surface. The springs are blue and cold!

Barbour's Map Turtle

Georgia Blind Cave Salamander

The shoals spider lily needs the shoals to survive.

Unusual Wildlife

The Flint has many special **habitats**. Habitats are places where plants and animals live. The Georgia blind cave salamander is **endemic** to the Flint River. It doesn't live anywhere else! Shoals spider lilies and Barbour's map turtles need shoals to survive. So does the tiny Halloween darter.

Halloween Darter

Farmers need the Flint to water their crops.

Appalachian Plateau
Blue Ridge Mountains
Valley and Ridge
Piedmont
★ Atlanta
Flint River
Upper Coastal Plain
Lower Coastal Plain
★ Albany
★ Bainbridge

Stormwater drains into the Flint River.

An Important Contribution

The Flint River does many important things. The river and its floodplains clean the **stormwater** from Atlanta. Stormwater runs off of dirty streets and parking lots when it rains. Farmers water their crops with water from the Flint. The river also provides water to cities like Albany and Bainbridge.

People need water to wash their cars.

People need water for their lawns.

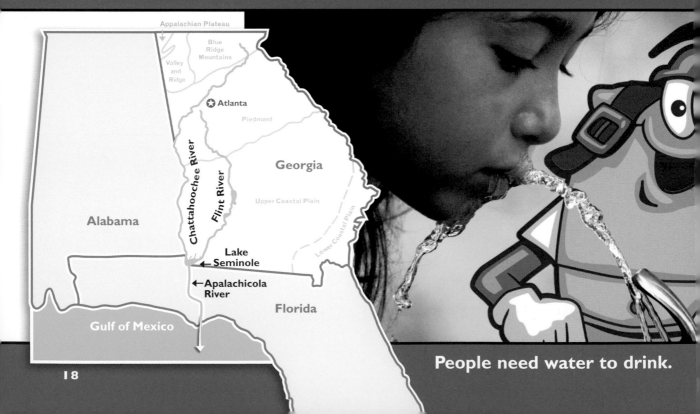

People need water to drink.

Problems Sharing the Water

The Flint River joins the Chattahoochee River at Lake Seminole. They form the Apalachicola River in Florida. It takes Georgia's water to the ocean. People in Georgia need the water. People in Florida need water, too. They cannot agree on how to share the water from Georgia.

People learn about the river at the Flint RiverQuarium.

Let's Keep it Beautiful

The Flint River is unusual, or different. It is one of a few rivers in the United States that flow freely for over 200 miles! People in Albany built the Flint RiverQuarium. The RiverQuarium helps them teach people about the Flint. They want to

Catfish

protect the river and keep it beautiful.

Glossary

blue hole springs – Caves or holes in limestone filled with groundwater that bubbles to the surface.

bluff – An area of high land.

caves – Holes in the ground.

dams – Structures on a river that block the water and form lakes.

endemic – Plants or animals that grow only in a certain place or habitat.

fall line – An area of land that falls steeply.

floodplains – Areas around a river that flood with water when it rains a lot.

groundwater – Water under the ground that seeps up to the surface.

habitats – Places where plants and animals live.

limestone – A type of rock.

natural – Places that people have not changed.

oxbow lakes – Curves in a river that get cut off and form lakes.

shoals – Shallow and rocky areas in a river.

stormwater – Water that runs off of streets and parking lots when it rains.

swamps – Wetlands that are covered with water all or most of the time.

wetlands – Areas that are covered with water all or some of the time.

Word Index

Image Credits

p. 4   Airport: © Lars Lindblad, iStockphoto.com; Groundwater: © Greg Greer, Marietta, Georgia

p. 6   Bluff aerial: Photo courtesy of Georgia Department of Economic Development; River: © Alan Cressler, Flickr.com; Kayaker: © Phil Berry, iStockphoto.com

p. 8   All: Photos courtesy of Georgia Department of Economic Development

p. 10   All: © Alan Cressler, Flickr.com

p. 12   Spring, Limestone bluff: © Alan Cressler, Flickr.com; Lake Blackshear: Photo courtesy of Georgia Department of Economic Development

p. 14   Spider lily, Salamander: © Alan Cressler, Flickr.com; Turtle: © Greg Greer, Marietta, Georgia

p. 15   Darter: Photo courtesy of the University of Georgia, Odum School of Ecology

p. 16   Stormwater: © John Hallett, iStockphoto.com; Irrigation: © Dave Willman, iStockphoto.com

p. 18   Lawn watering: © Frances Twitty, iStockphoto.com; Car washing: © Blade Kostas, iStockphoto.com; Drinking: © Rob Friedman, iStockphoto.com

p. 20   Aquarium Interior: © Flint RiverQuarium; Aquarium exterior: Photographer unknown, Wikipedia.com

p. 21   Catfish: © Matt Matthews, iStockphoto.com

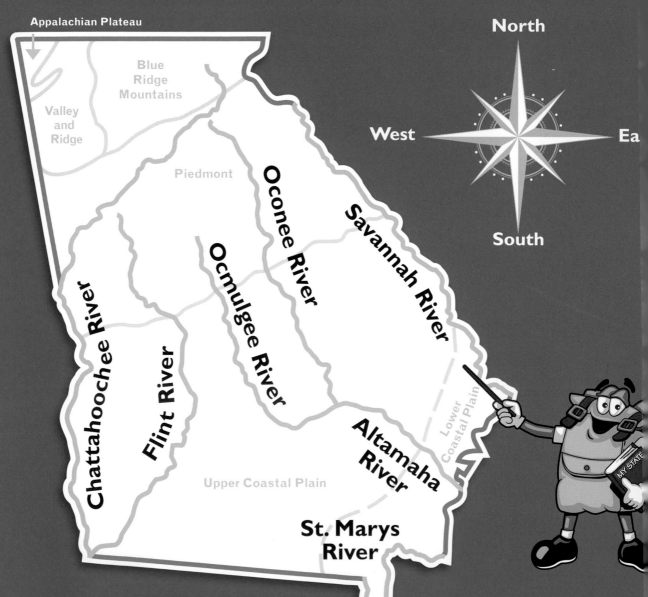

Appalachian Plateau

Blue
Ridge
Mountains

Valley
and
Ridge

Piedmont

Oconee River

Savannah River

Ocmulgee River

Chattahoochee River

Flint River

North

West

Ea

South

Lower
Coastal Plain

Altamaha
River

Upper Coastal Plain

St. Marys
River